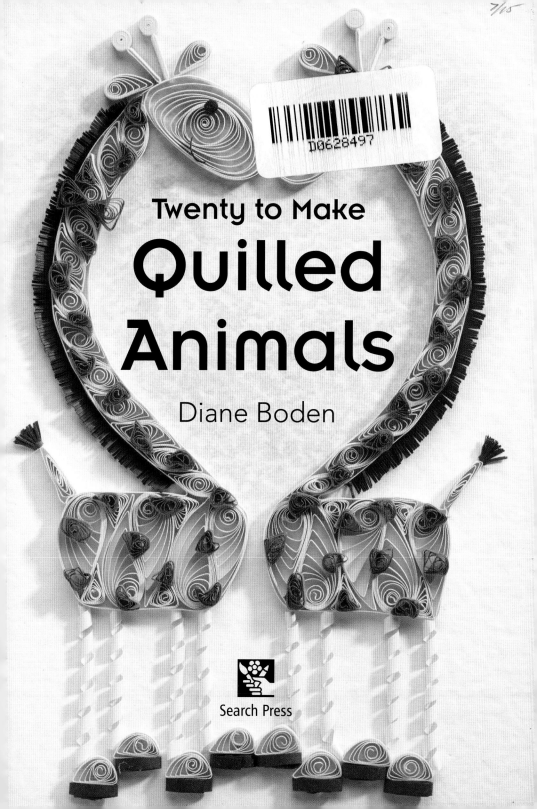

Twenty to Make
Quilled
Animals

Diane Boden

Search Press

First published in 2015

Search Press Limited
Wellwood, North Farm Road,
Tunbridge Wells, Kent TN2 3DR

Text copyright © Diane Boden 2015

Photographs by Paul Bricknell at
Search Press Studios

Photographs and design copyright
© Search Press Ltd 2015

Print ISBN: 978-1-78221-088-7
ebook ISBN: 978-1-78126-235-1

Suppliers
If you have difficulty in obtaining any of the
materials and equipment mentioned in this book,
then please visit the Search Press website for
details of suppliers: www.searchpress.com

Printed in China

Dedication

*I would like to dedicate this book to
my dear husband Tris, who plied me with
endless cups of tea during long quilling sessions,
and to my Wednesday afternoon quilling ladies
for sacrificing classes so I could finish the book!*

*'In His hand is the life of every creature
and the breath of all mankind.'*
Job 12 v.10

Contents

Introduction

What I love most about quilling is that it is such a versatile craft – virtually any subject matter can be represented by simply rolling up narrow strips of paper into coils, then forming them into any number of different shapes. The diversity of the animal kingdom has been the inspiration for this fun collection of designs – everything from a baby panda about to tuck into a bamboo shoot to a pair of romantic giraffes!

Basic quilling methods have been used to make the majority of the projects – easier ones first, moving through to those using more challenging techniques in order to create fluffy tails and spiky hedgehog spines. The designs may be adapted for different uses – many would lend themselves to greetings cards, for example. If a design is too large for your purpose, simply halve the strip measurements given and the design should still work out.

Remember that quilling is a bit like knitting in that tension plays an important role; make sure you give your coils room to 'breathe' by not rolling them too tightly. This will make it easier to shape the coils for the sections required.

Whatever you choose to make, whether it be a lion's mane or an alpaca's fringe, enjoy the simple pleasure of rolling your strips to bring this paper menagerie to life.

Diane Boden

4

Tools and materials

Tools:

You will need these basic tools and materials for most of the projects in this book.

A **quilling tool** has a wooden, metal or plastic handle and a metal end with a slot in it, through which you thread the quilling paper or strips.

A pair of **small, sharp scissors** is useful for cutting quilling paper and card.

PVA glue in a bottle with a **fine-tipped applicator** is used for sticking the quilling paper together and sticking designs down onto card. It should be used sparingly.

You will need a **ruler** to measure out your quilling papers.

A **cutting mat** protects the surface on which you are working. Many have gridlines to help achieve straight edges.

A **pencil** is useful for when you need to mark out a template.

Tracing paper can be used for making templates and the **cellophane** from a window envelope can help to create eccentric circles (see opposite).

Cocktail sticks are useful for neatening pegs and for picking up finished coils.

Some quillers find **tweezers** helpful for positioning small coils.

Use a **fine black pen** to draw facial details on your designs.

Materials:

Quilling papers are more usually referred to as '**quilling strips**', the most popular width being 3mm (1/8in).

Card can be used for backgrounds and is available in different weights and colours.

Chalk pastels are useful for shading card backgrounds to enhance your designs.

Techniques

Introduction

The art of quilling, or coiling paper, consists of rolling narrow strips of special paper to create decorative designs using a quilling tool. The coil is then released, glued at the tip and shaped. These shaped coils are arranged to form flowers, leaves, and other ornamental shapes.

Eccentric circles

This technique is useful for organising the loops within a coil, and enables a coil to be shaped without losing the effect. Make a coil using a 3mm (¹/₈in) wide strip. Glue down the end to make the size of coil you want (see 1). Insert the quilling tool back into the centre and rewind the coil quite firmly – this should bring in the excess paper which gathers at the edge of the strip, and creates an ugly 'collar'. As you relax tension on the quilling tool, gently pay out the coil, and encourage the centre of the coil over to the edge (see 2). Hold it in your fingers, then place a small amount of glue on to a smooth surface, such as a tile or piece of cellophane (such as that in a 'window' envelope). Carefully lay the coil on the glue and hold it there until it dries. Gently lift off the coil, which is now ready to use. It can be shaped further, depending on the design (see 3).

1　　**2**　　**3**

Pegs and tight coils

A peg is a tight coil made with a quilling tool (see below). When the end of the strip is reached, it is glued down. A finished peg can be neatened in two ways: by applying pressure to smooth it out, and by inserting a cocktail stick into the centre and twisting to create a neat hole. A tight coil is formed without the use of a quilling tool. The strip is curled over at the very end and rolled tightly on itself so that there is no hole in the centre, and is useful when making faces and snouts (see Reindeer nose, page 42).

Pointed fringed flowers

This technique is used in the Hedgehog design (see page 40). Cut a series of points along a 5mm (¼in) wide strip. Cut two strips of paper at a time, by holding them exactly one on top of the other. Glue the top strip 2mm (¹/₁₆in) in from the strip underneath to make it easier to insert into the quilling tool. Roll up the strips. If the ends are uneven when you reach the end, trim one back to make it easier to glue down. Coat the base with glue and allow it to dry. Peel back the points to reveal the flower.

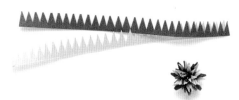

Long fringing

This technique is used in the Fox and Squirrel designs (see pages 32 and 34). Cut a fringe along a 5mm (¼in) wide strip. Insert the fringed strip in the quilling tool and begin to roll, but instead of rolling the paper on itself, begin to travel down the tool a little at a time, so that the fringing grows in length. Apply a small spot of glue at intervals to keep it together. When you reach the end, carefully remove it from the tool and allow to dry. Roll two fringed strips of different colours together for a mottled effect.

Sheep

Materials:

Quilling papers: 3mm (¹/₈in) strips in cream, and mid-brown; 2mm (¹/₁₆in) strips in white, yellow and green; 5mm (¼in) strips in cream or white

Small piece of white or cream paper

White background card

Green chalk pastel

Tools:

Quilling tool

Small, sharp scissors

PVA glue

Ruler

Fine black pen

Instructions:

1 To make the head, join together three 45cm (17¾in) mid-brown strips end to end and make a solid coil. Dome the coil slightly by pushing gently from below, coat the underside with glue, then allow to dry.

2 For the body, using 3mm (¹/₈in) cream paper, make twenty coils from 11cm (4¼in) strips, twenty coils from 7.5cm (3in) strips, and fifteen coils from 5.5cm (2¼in) strips.

3 For the ears, make two coils from 7.5cm (3in) mid-brown strips. Pinch into teardrop shapes.

4 To make the feet, make two coils from 11cm (4¼in) mid-brown strips. Pinch into rounded shapes with a flat base.

5 For the topknot, make a fringed flower from a 7.5cm (3in) strip of 5mm (¼in) wide cream or white paper.

6 Make two pegs for the eyes from 3cm (1¼in) strips of 2mm (¹/₁₆in) wide white paper. Mark the pupils with a fine black pen.

7 For the mouth, glue two short strips of mid-brown paper together to make a firmer strip, then curve to form a mouth.

8 To assemble the sheep, shade the background card with the chalk pastel. Then cut a 4cm (1½in) diameter circle from a piece of white or cream paper. Glue 11cm (4¼in) coils and 7.5cm (3in) coils alternately around the edge of the paper circle, half on and half off. Fill the centre with the remaining coils. Where gaps occur, glue more coils on top to cover them. Glue the card circle to the background card.

9 Make some coils from 3.5cm (1³/₈in) white strips of 2mm (¹/₁₆in) paper for the flowers. Pinch into teardrop shapes. Glue six teardrops together to make a flower. Make tight coils from 3.5cm (1³/₈in) yellow strips 2mm (¹/₁₆in) wide for the flower centres. Make some leaves from 3.5cm (1³/₈in) green strips 2mm (¹/₁₆in) wide, pinching either end to make the leaf shape. Assemble the flowers and glue them around the sheep as shown.

This alternative black sheep uses brown papers for the wool. You can try using half mid-brown and half darker brown rolled together. Make the head, ears and feet from darker brown strips. See the detail opposite (bottom right).

Bunny

Materials:

Quilling papers: 3mm (^{1}/$_8$in) strips in dark grey, pale pink and white; 2mm (^{1}/$_{16}$in) strips in white

Green background card

Green chalk pastel

Tools:

Quilling tool

Small, sharp scissors

PVA glue

Ruler

Fine black pen

Instructions:

1 To make the head, join one 45cm (17¾in) dark grey strip to one 22.5cm (8⅞in) dark grey strip end to end and roll into a coil. Make into an eccentric circle.

2 For the body, join three 45cm (17¾in) dark grey strips end to end and roll into a large coil. Make into an eccentric circle.

3 For the ears, join a 22.5cm (8⅞in) pale pink strip to a 22.5cm (8⅞in) dark grey strip, then roll from the pink end. Pinch into an ear shape.

4 Make two 11cm (4¼in) dark grey coils and pinch into semicircles for the paws.

5 For the nose, make a pale pink coil from a 5.5cm (2¼in) pink strip and pinch it into a heart shape.

6 To make the eyes, roll two 7.5cm (3in) ovals from 2mm (^{1}/$_{16}$in) pale pink strips. Draw on pupils with a fine black pen.

7 Take a short 2mm (^{1}/$_{16}$in) strip of white paper and cut narrow strips into it at both ends. Splay out the individual whiskers.

8 Shade the background card with the chalk pastel and glue down the bunny as shown.

9 To make the 'Bunnies and Carrots' Noughts and Crosses game, make some bunnies as above using different shades of brown strips, with orange and green for the carrots.

10 For the bunnies facing the other way, make the ears using one 45cm (17¾in) strip of your chosen colour.

11 To make the tail, use a 3mm (^{1}/$_8$in) white strip and make a 5.5cm (2¼in) length of fringing. Roll into a fringed flower and open out. Glue to the back of the body.

12 To make a carrot, join two 45cm (17¾in) orange strips end to end, and roll into a coil. Pinch firmly to make a long, pointed shape.

13 Make three 11cm (4¼in) strip coils in green and pinch into thin, pointed shapes for the leaves.

14 To assemble, glue the bunnies and carrots onto separate small cards 5cm (2in) square.

15 Make up a grid on a square piece of card using 5mm (¼in) wide strips.

16 You are now ready for a game of 'Bunnies and Carrots'.

Make a cute bunny like this and use it as a card or picture. For the alternative Bunnies and Carrots game (opposite), follow steps 9 to 16.

Dog

Materials:

Quilling papers: 3mm (¹/₈in) strips in light brown, black, white, pale pink, gold edge and a scrap of red; 2mm (¹/₁₆in) strips in black

Beige background card

Light brown chalk pastel

Tools:

Quilling tool

Small, sharp scissors

PVA glue

Ruler

Instructions:

1 To make the head, join together two 45cm (17¾in) light brown strips and one 22.5cm (8⁷/₈in) light brown strip end to end and roll into a large coil. Make this into an eccentric circle.

2 For the body, join together four 45cm (17¾in) light brown strips end to end and roll into a large coil. Make this into an eccentric circle, then pinch into shape as shown.

3 Make two coils from 22.5cm (8⁷/₈in) light brown strips. Pinch into ear shapes as shown.

4 For the nose, make a fairly tight coil from a 15cm (6in) black strip. Pinch into an oval shape.

5 Make two pegs for the eyes from 5.5cm (2¼in) black strips. Edge the eyes a couple of times with a short, white strip.

6 Make a curved shape from a 7.5cm (3in) pale pink coil for the tongue.

7 For the neck, make a triangle from an 11cm (4¼in) light brown strip.

8 Make a very loose coil from a 30cm (11¾in) light brown strip for the tail. Pinch into a point at one end, and fit to the side of the dog's body at the other end.

9 For the paw, make a semicircle from a 22.5cm (8⁷/₈in) light brown strip.

10 For the leg outline roll a large, loose coil from a 22.5cm (8⁷/₈in) light brown strip. Then pinch it into a long, thin curved shape.

11 Cut a short, red strip to fit around the dog's neck for the collar.

12 To make the collar tag, roll a solid coil from an 11cm (4¼in) gold edge strip.

13 For the bone, make a rectangle from a 15cm (6in) white strip. For the ends, roll two 11cm (4¼in) coils and pinch into kidney shapes. Glue together, then glue a strip around the whole bone to define the shape.

14 To assemble, shade the background card with the chalk pastel, then glue down the dog as shown, adding the bone by his paw. For the wagging tail effect, make four 5.5cm (2¼in) thin crescents from 2mm (¹/₁₆in) wide black strips and glue them around the tail as shown.

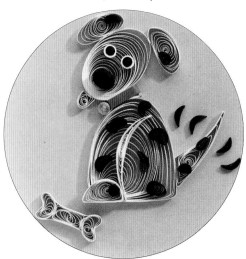

Spotty Dog

*For the alternative spotty dog (opposite, left and top),
make a dog in white. Then add the spots by making ten
5cm (2in) coils from 2mm (¹/₁₆in) wide black strips. Shape
them into irregular ovals and glue them on as shown.*

Donkey

Materials:

Quilling papers: 3mm (1/8in) strips in dark grey, black, light grey, white, pale pink and pale gold

Beige background card

Light brown chalk pastel

Tools:

Quilling tool

Small, sharp scissors

PVA glue

Ruler

Instructions:

1 To make the head, join a 45cm (17¾in) dark grey strip to a 22.5cm (8⁷/₈in) dark grey strip end to end and roll into a large coil, then pinch into an oval. Make this into an eccentric circle.

2 For the muzzle, roll a 30cm (11¾in) light grey strip into a coil, and pinch into a crescent shape. Glue the crescent to the oval, and glue a dark grey strip around both shapes.

3 For the ears, make two petal shapes from 22.5cm (8⁷/₈in) dark grey strips. Make two shapes from 15cm (6in) pale pink strips. Glue the grey and pink shapes together and edge with a dark grey strip as shown.

4 Make two pegs from 5.5cm (2¼in) black strips for the eyes. Edge round a few times with a white strip.

5 For the mane, make eight 7.5cm (3in) triangles from black strips – four for the top of the head and four for the neck.

6 To make the neck, make a shaped rectangle from a 15cm (6in) dark grey strip.

7 Make five petal shapes from 30cm (11¾in) dark grey strips for the body.

8 For the tail, make three thin eye shapes from 15cm (6in) dark grey strips, and a long, thin shape from a 7.5cm (3in) strip.

9 Make four petal shapes from 22.5cm (8⁷/₈in) dark grey strips for the legs.

10 For the hooves, make four coils from 11cm (4¼in) black strips and shape as shown.

11 To assemble, shade the background card with the chalk pastel, then glue down all the shapes. Squash the body shapes together when sticking them down. If there are any large gaps between the body sections, make a few extra triangles and insert them in the spaces as shown. Outline the body with another strip to define the shape, before sticking on the legs, tail, mane and ears.

12 For the straw, make some thin shapes using 11cm (4¼in) pale gold strips as shown. Glue a few in the donkey's mouth, and some around the hooves to finish.

Flying Pigs

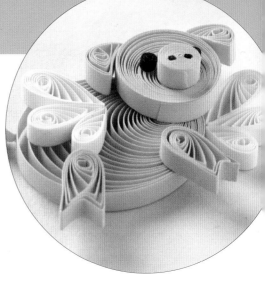

Materials:

Quilling papers: 3mm
(¹/₈in) strips in pale
peach and white;
2mm (¹/₁₆in) strips
in black

White background card

Pale blue chalk pastel

Tools:

Quilling tool

Small, sharp scissors

PVA glue

Ruler

Fine black pen

Cocktail stick

Pencil

Instructions:

1 To make the head, join a 45cm (17¾in) strip to a 22.5cm (8⁷/₈in) strip in pale peach end to end and make a large coil. Make this into an eccentric circle.

2 For the snout, make a tight coil using a 22.5cm (8⁷/₈in) pale peach strip.

3 Join two 45cm (17¾in) pale peach strips end to end and roll into a large coil for the body. Make this into an eccentric circle.

4 For the trotters, make two coils from 15cm (6in) pale peach strips. Pinch into a thin shape rounded at one end. Make a dent at the other end to form the shape of the trotters.

5 Make two coils from 7.5cm (3in) pale peach strips. Form into rounded triangles for the ears.

6 For the wings, make two teardrops from 15cm (6in) white strips, two more from 11cm (4¼in) white strips, and a third pair from 7.5cm (3in) white strips.

7 Roll two pegs from 3cm (1¼in) black strips 2mm (¹/₁₆in) wide for the eyes.

8 To assemble, glue the head to the body over the full end of the eccentric circle. Attach the eyes and snout to the head. Draw dots on the snout with a fine black pen. Then glue on both sets of wings, trotters and ears.

9 Make a curly tail by winding a short 2mm (¹/₁₆in) strip around a cocktail stick. Trim to size, then glue to the body.

10 For the background, trace the enlarged cloud stencil using the template below onto a scrap of card, and cut it out. Using this as a guide, move it around the white background card and colour around it with the chalk pastel to make a cloudy sky.

11 To finish, glue down the flying pigs.

*Cloud template:
enlarge to 200%*

Hippo

Materials:

Quilling papers: 3mm
($^{1}/_{8}$in) strips in lavender,
black, white and lilac
edge; 2mm ($^{1}/_{16}$in)
strips in yellow, white
and green

White background card

Scrap of white paper

Pale green chalk pastel

Tools:

Quilling tool

Small, sharp
scissors

PVA glue

Ruler

Instructions:

1 For the body, make approximately forty-five petal shapes from 15cm (6in) lavender strips.

2 For the head, make six 22.5cm (8$^{7}/_{8}$in) petal shapes, and two 15cm (6in) petal shapes from lavender strips.

3 Make two 11cm (4¼in) teardrops from lavender strips for the ears.

4 For the legs, make two 22.5cm (8$^{7}/_{8}$in) shaped rectangles and one 11cm (4¼in) strip thin rectangle, all in lavender.

5 Make five semicircles from 2mm ($^{1}/_{16}$in) white strips for the toenails.

6 For the tail, make a petal shape from a 7.5cm (3in) lavender strip. Glue four short strips together to make a firmer strip, trim to size and glue one end to the petal shape.

7 For the eye, make a 5.5cm (2¼in) oval shape from a black strip. Outline it a couple of times with a white strip.

8 To make the mouth, glue together three short black strips, then curve and trim.

9 For the tutu, make twelve 15cm (6in) teardrops from lilac-edged strips. Wind a 3mm ($^{1}/_{8}$in) wide white strip three times round each teardrop. Make eleven pegs from 4.5cm (1¾in) white strips.

10 Trace the enlarged hippo template onto a piece of white paper. Glue down the shapes using the template as a guide. Cut round the template, close to the quilled shapes and outline the hippo with a strip of lavender to

define the shape. Then glue down the ears and tail.

11 Make the tutu by arranging the teardrops and pegs alternately around the middle of the hippo. Glue down a strip of lilac to edge the pegs and define the tutu shape.

12 For the flowers, use 2mm ($^{1}/_{16}$in) wide strips, and make six petals for each flower with 4cm (1½in) length strips. For the centres, make pegs from 4cm (1½in) length yellow strips. For the leaves, make green coils from 4cm (1½in) strips and pinch the ends to make leaf shapes. For the flower stems, glue together three green strips to make one firmer strip.

13 Glue one flower to the hippo's ear, one to her mouth by the stem, and arrange the others to either side.

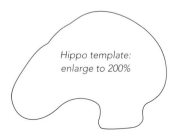

*Hippo template:
enlarge to 200%*

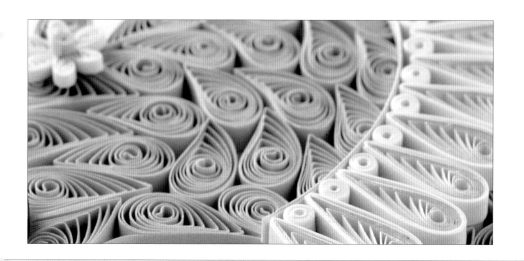

Cat

Materials:

Quilling papers: 3mm (¹⁄₈in) strips in black, light grey, pale pink, and white; 2mm (¹⁄₁₆in) strips in light grey

Small piece of thin white card

Beige background card

Grey and pink chalk pastels

Tools:

Quilling tool

Small, sharp scissors

PVA glue

Ruler

Instructions:

1 Enlarge and trace the body and tail templates and cut out from the thin white card. If desired, colour the edges of the body and tail with grey chalk pastel as shown.

2 To make the ears, join a 5.5cm (2¼in) pale pink strip to a 5.5cm (2¼in) black strip. Roll from the pink end to make a coil, then pinch into a triangle.

3 For the eyes, make two pegs from 5.5cm (2¼in) black strips.

4 For the nose, make a coil from a 5.5cm (2¼in) pale pink strip and shape into a triangle.

5 Make two pegs from 5.5cm (2¼in) pale pink strips for the cheeks.

6 For the mouth, make a double thickness pale pink strip and trim to size.

7 For the whiskers, make a double thickness strip from 2mm (¹⁄₁₆in) light grey paper and fold in half. Glue another strip for the centre whisker and trim to size as shown.

8 To make the head markings, make three triangles from 5.5cm (2¼in) black strips.

9 For the body markings, make six triangles from 7.5cm (3in) black strips.

10 Make ten 4.5cm triangles from black strips for the tail markings.

11 To make the paws, make two semicircles from 22.5cm (8⁷⁄₈in) white strips. Outline them a couple of times with black strips.

12 Make four 5.5cm (2¼in) teardrop shapes from 2mm (¹⁄₁₆in) light grey strips for the claws.

13 To assemble, glue all sections to the body and tail templates, except for the ears. Glue a black strip all round the body, beginning at the side of one paw, to define the shape. Glue another strip around the tail section. Then glue on the ears and tail. Shade the background card with the pink chalk pastel, then glue down the completed cat.

Cat and tail template:
enlarge to 200%

For the variation (below and opposite), make the cat as for the black one, using dark and light orange paper instead of black, on yellow background card. Position the tail to one side as shown, instead of hanging down.

Pandas

Materials:

Quilling papers: 3mm (1/8in) strips in black and white; 2mm (1/16in) strips in pale pink and green

Light brown background card

Tools:

Quilling tool

Small, sharp scissors

PVA glue

Ruler

Instructions:

1 To make the body for the large panda, join five 45cm (17¾in) white strips end to end and roll into a large coil. Make this into an eccentric circle.

2 For the head, join three 45cm (17¾in) white strips end to end and make a large coil. Make this into an eccentric circle.

3 Make two 15cm (6in) semicircles from black strips for the ears.

4 For the eyes, make two 5.5cm (2¼in) black pegs pinched into an oval. Outline with a 5.5cm (2¼in) white strip, then add an 11cm (4¼in) black strip to complete the eye.

5 Make a 5.5cm (2¼in) black triangle for the nose.

6 To make the arm holding the branch, make a 30cm (11¾in) thin oval coil from a black strip. For the other arm, make a 15cm (6in) semicircle in black.

7 For the feet, make two 30cm (11¾in) fairly tight coils in black, pinched into an oval.

8 To make the pads, make two 22.5cm (8⁷/₈in) and six 5.5cm (2¼in) oval shapes from 2mm (1/16in) pale pink strips. Glue these on to the feet as shown.

9 For the leaves, make seven 11cm (4¼in) pointed eye shapes from 2mm (1/16in) green strips. Glue two strips together to make a firmer strip for the stem.

10 Glue everything down onto the background card as shown.

11 For the medium panda, make as above using the following measurements:

Body: two 45cm (17¾in) strips joined to one 22.5cm (8⁷/₈in) strip.

Head: one 45cm (17¾in) strip joined to one 22.5cm (8⁷/₈in) strip.

Ears: two 11cm (4¼in) semicircles.

Eyes: two 4cm (1½in) black oval pegs, outlined with a 4cm (1½in) white strip, then a 7.5cm (3in) black strip.

Nose: one 4cm (1½in) triangle.

Arms: two 15cm (6in) semicircles.

Feet: two 15cm (6in) ovals.

Pads: two 7.5cm (3in) heart shapes.

12 For the baby panda, make as above using the following measurements:

Body: one 45cm (17¾in) strip.

Head: one 45cm (17¾in) strip.

Ears: two 7.5cm (3in) strips.

Eyes: two 2cm black pegs, two 2cm strips of white, and two 7.5cm (3in) strips of black.

Nose: one 3cm (1¼in) triangle.

Arms: two 7.5cm (3in).

Feet: two 11cm (4¼in) ovals.

Pads: two 5.5cm (2¼in) heart shapes.

Lion

Materials:

Quilling papers: 3mm (⅛in) strips in pale gold, deep gold, black, white, brown and green

Pale yellow background card

Pale yellow chalk pastel

Tools:

Quilling tool

Small, sharp scissors

PVA glue

Ruler

Instructions:

1 To make the head, join five 45cm (17¾in) pale gold strips end to end and make a large coil. Do not allow it to open up too much. Pinch into a slight oval shape.

2 For the body, make eight 15cm (6in) petal shapes, one 15cm (6in) teardrop, two 11cm (4¼in) teardrops and two 11cm (4¼in) triangles using pale gold strips.

3 For the mane, make approximately twenty 11cm (4¼in) petal shapes and six 7.5cm (3in) petal shapes using the deep gold strips.

4 Make two semicircles from 22.5cm (8⅞in) pale gold strips for the ears.

5 For the eyes, make two ovals from 7.5cm (3in) black strips, then add a 5.5cm (2¼in) white strip round the outside as shown.

6 For the muzzle, make a triangle from a 22.5cm (8⅞in) pale gold strip.

7 Add the nose by making a triangle from a 7.5cm (3in) black strip.

8 For the legs, make two coils from 30cm (11¾in) pale gold strips. Pinch into shapes that will fit the sides of the lion.

9 For the front of the paws, make two 22.5cm (8⅞in) teardrops and four 22.5cm (8⅞in) curved petal shapes for the sides of the paws from pale gold strips.

10 For each of the four claws, glue six short brown strips together and trim to size.

11 For the tail, make a 15cm (6in) petal shape from the deep gold strips and a thin coil from a 15cm (6in) strip of pale gold.

12 To assemble, shade the background card, position all sections of the lion, then begin by sticking down the head, ears and mane. Add the body sections, then the legs and the paw sections. Glue a strip of pale gold around the body, legs and paws to define the shape. Glue on the tail and features to finish the lion.

13 Make some grass from 15cm (6in), 11cm (4¼in) and 7.5cm (3in) green strips and glue them either side of the lion as shown.

Monkey

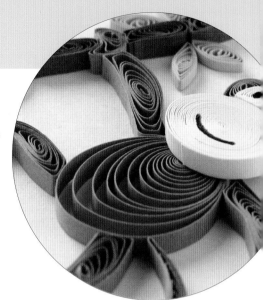

Materials:

Quilling papers: 3mm (¹/₈in) strips in brown, ivory, green and mid-brown; 2mm (¹/₁₆in) strips in black

Cream background card

Yellow chalk pastel

Tools:

Quilling tool

Small, sharp scissors

PVA glue

Ruler

Instructions:

1 To make the head, roll a coil using a 45cm (17¾in) brown strip. Make this into an eccentric circle.

2 For the ears, make two 15cm (6in) brown strips into semicircles.

3 For the mouth section, join together four 45cm (17¾in) ivory strips end to end and roll to make a fairly tight coil. Pinch into an oval shape.

4 Glue together three short black strips of 2mm (¹/₁₆in) wide paper, trim and curve into a mouth shape.

5 For the face, make two shapes from 15cm (6in) ivory strips rolled into fairly tight ovals and then shaped with one flat end as shown.

6 Make two 5.5cm (2¼in) ovals from 2mm (¹/₁₆in) black strips for the eyes and glue them to the face.

7 To make the body, join two 45cm (17¾in) brown strips end to end, plus another 22.5cm (8⁷/₈in) strip. Roll into a large coil and make into an eccentric circle.

8 For the arms and legs, make four loose coils from 45cm (17¾in) brown strips. Pinch into long, thin shapes as shown.

9 Make four curved shapes from 15cm (6in) brown coils for the hands and feet, as shown.

10 For the tail, roll a loose coil from a 45cm (17¾in) brown strip and pinch into a long, thin shape that is pointed at both ends.

11 To make the branch, make three sausage shapes from 22.5cm (8⁷/₈in) mid-brown strips. Make nine leaves from 15cm (6in) green strips.

12 To assemble, shade the background card with the chalk pastel, then glue down all the shapes. The mouth and face sections are glued on top of the head and body.

Gift Tag

To make the monkey gift tag (opposite, bottom), simply halve all the measurements given for the original monkey, use mid-brown paper and glue to an oval cardboard tag. Use a short strip of mid-brown paper to make the hanger.

Alpaca

Materials:

Quilling papers: 3mm (^{1}/$_8$in) strips in beige, mid-brown and black; 5mm (¼in) strips in beige (for the topknot only); 2mm (^{1}/$_{16}$in) strips in green

Pale green background card

Green chalk pastel

Tools:

Quilling tool

Small, sharp scissors

PVA glue

Ruler

Instructions:

1 To make the head, join six 45cm (17¾in) beige strips end to end and roll into a fairly tight coil. Pinch into a slight oval shape.

2 For the front of the face, roll one 45cm (17¾in) beige strip into a fairly tight coil and pinch it into a thin oval. Glue to the head.

3 For the neck, make seven petal shapes from 15cm (6in) beige strips.

4 For the body, make nine large petal shapes from 45cm (17¾in) beige strips.

5 To make the tail, make a petal shape from a 15cm (6in) beige strip.

6 For the legs, make eight coils from 30cm (11¾in) beige strips and pinch into shape.

7 Make four coils from 11cm (4¼in) mid-brown strips for the hooves and pinch into shape.

8 For the ears, make two triangles from 15cm (6in) beige coils.

9 Make a triangle from a 3cm (1¼in) long black strip for the nose.

10 For the eyes, make two small ovals from 5.5cm (2¼in) black strips.

11 Glue two short black strips together, fold in half and glue about a third of the way along from the fold – then curve the free ends round to form a mouth and trim if necessary.

12 To make the topknot, make three fringed flowers from 11cm (4¼in) strips of 5mm (¼in) wide beige paper.

13 To assemble, shade the background card and then glue the head and neck shapes to it. Add the body sections and squash them up next to each other as you glue them down.

14 Add the leg sections, then glue a 3mm (^{1}/$_8$in) beige strip all round the alpaca to define the shape.

15 Glue down the ears, tail and hooves; then glue the fringed flowers and features to the face.

16 If there are any gaps in the body or neck, roll some tiny beige coils from 3mm (^{1}/$_8$in) strips and insert them into the spaces.

17 Make a number of tiny coils from 2mm (^{1}/$_{16}$in) green strips (there is no need to glue down the free ends) and glue them randomly around the hooves to represent grass.

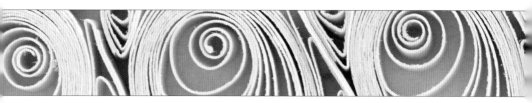

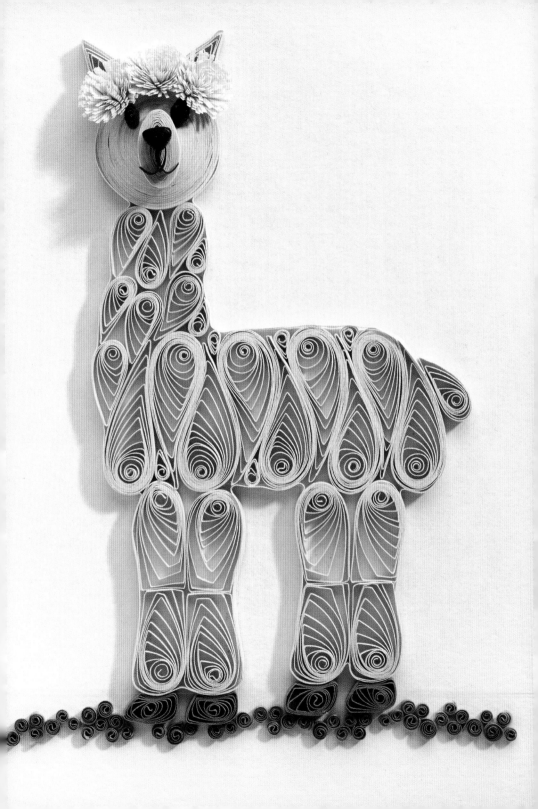

Elephant

Materials:

Quilling papers: 3mm (¹⁄₈in) strips in pale, medium and dark pink, and ivory; 2mm (¹⁄₁₆in) strips in dark grey

White background card

Pink chalk pastels in three shades

Tools:

Quilling tool

Small, sharp scissors

PVA glue

Ruler

Instructions:

1 To make the body, join three 45cm (17¾in) strips in dark pink end to end. Roll up into a large coil and make an eccentric circle.

2 For the head, join two 45cm (17¾in) dark pink strips end to end. Roll up into a large coil and make an eccentric circle.

3 To make the ear, make a coil from a 45cm (17¾in) dark pink strip. Make this into an eccentric circle, and shape into an ear.

4 For the legs, make two shaped rectangles from 22.5cm (8⁷⁄₈in) dark pink strips.

5 To make the trunk, make a coil from a 30cm (11¾in) dark pink strip. Pinch into a shape that will fit around the head at one end, and curls round at the other end.

6 Make a peg from a 4cm (1½in) dark grey 2mm (¹⁄₁₆in) strip for the eye.

7 For the tusk, make a small curved triangle from a 5.5cm (2¼in) ivory strip.

8 Make a thin, pointed shape from an 11cm (4¼in) dark pink strip for the tail.

9 To assemble, shade the background card and glue on all shapes except for the ear and tail. Glue a dark pink strip all round the elephant to define the shape. Glue on the tail and ear. Make two more elephants using the other shades of pink and assemble as before.

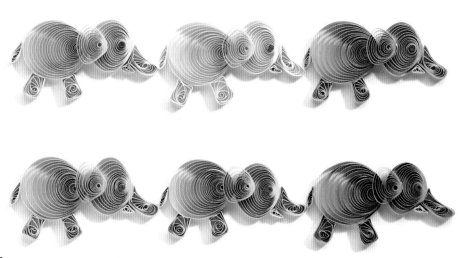

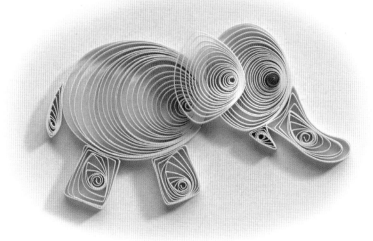

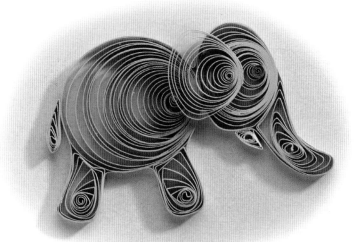

Tiny Coloured Elephants

To make these alternatives (opposite), halve the measurements given for the pink elephants, with the exception of the tusk, which is a 3cm (1¼in) long strip. Assemble as for the pink elephants and glue them, trunk to tail, on the background card.

Fox

Materials:

Quilling papers: 3mm ($^1/_8$in) strips in reddish brown, white, black and green; 2mm ($^1/_{16}$in) strips in black; 5mm (¼in) strips in white and reddish brown (for the tail only)

Pale green background card

Green chalk pastel

Tools:

Quilling tool

Small, sharp scissors

PVA glue

Ruler

Instructions:

1 To make the upper head, make four shaped triangles from 15cm (6in) reddish brown strips. Make one teardrop from a 15cm (6in) white strip.

2 For the lower head, make four petal shapes from 15cm (6in) white strips, and two petal shapes from 22.5cm (8$^7/_8$in) white strips.

3 Make a triangle from a 5.5cm (2¼in) black strip for the nose.

4 Glue two short black strips together and fold into a 'v' shape for the mouth. Trim to size and glue to the bottom point of the nose.

5 For the eyes, make two very thin crescents from 3.5cm (1$^3/_8$in) black strips 2mm ($^1/_{16}$in) wide.

6 To make the body, make a large coil from a 45cm (17¾in) reddish brown strip, joined to a 22.5cm (8$^7/_8$in) strip. Pinch into a shape with a curved side and a flat side as shown.

7 For the ears, make two triangles from 11cm (4¼in) white strips, and the same from 11cm (4¼in) reddish brown strips. Glue together, and outline the ears with a reddish brown strip.

8 For the tail, make three long, fringed strips (see page 7) from 7.5cm (3in) strips of 5mm (¼in) white, and three long, fringed strips from 11cm (4¼in) of 5mm (¼in) reddish brown.

9 To assemble, shade the background card and glue on the shapes, beginning with the head sections, then the body. Glue a reddish brown strip around the head and body, before sticking down the ears. Finally, glue down the tail sections, beginning with the white fringing.

10 For the leaves, make twenty-two 9cm (3½in) eye shapes from green strips. Glue two green strips together to make a firmer strip for a stem; make a second stem. Curve the stems on either side of the fox and arrange on the background with the leaves, before sticking them down.

Grey Squirrel

Materials:

Quilling papers: 3mm ($^1/_8$in) strips in light grey, white, pale pink, green and brown; 2mm ($^1/_{16}$in) strips in black; 5mm ($^1/_4$in) strips in white and grey (for the tail only) and various shades of brown

Beige background card

Brown chalk pastel

Tools:

Quilling tool

Small, sharp scissors

PVA glue

Ruler

Instructions:

1 To make the head, make a coil from a 45cm (17¾in) grey strip. Pinch into shape as shown.

2 For the ears, make two coils from 7.5cm (3in) grey strips and pinch into triangles.

3 Make a tiny coil for the nose from a 4cm (1½in) pale pink strip and pinch into a triangle.

4 For the eye, make a tiny coil from a 3cm (1¼in) black strip 2mm ($^1/_{16}$in) wide.

5 To make the throat, make a small coil from a 7.5cm (3in) white strip and pinch into shape.

6 For the front of the body, make two large coils from 45cm (17¾in) white strips. Pinch into shape as shown.

7 For the large leg, make a coil from a 45cm (17¾in) light grey strip and pinch into a large petal shape.

8 For the small leg, make a coil from a 22.5cm (8$^7/_8$in) grey strip and pinch into a crescent shape.

9 To make the feet, make two coils from 22.5cm (8$^7/_8$in) grey strips and pinch into semicircles.

10 For the large arm, make a coil from a 30cm (11¾in) grey strip. Pinch into shape as shown.

11 For the small arm, make a coil from a 15cm (6in) grey strip and pinch into a curved triangle shape.

12 For the paws, make two 7.5cm (3in) coils and pinch into shape.

13 For the top half of the nut, using 3mm ($^1/_8$in) strips, roll a 7.5cm (3in) coil of green and pinch into shape. For the lower half, roll a coil from a 7.5cm (3in) strip of brown and pinch into a semicircle. Glue the shapes together and add a stalk from a double thickness strip of brown.

14 To make the tail, make twelve sections of long fringing (see page 7) using 5.5cm (2¼in) strips of 5mm (¼in) white and grey, rolled together down the quiling tool.

15 To assemble, shade the background card and place all sections on the background. Glue the tip of the tail first, then work down to the base of the tail. Glue down the back sections of the squirrel and fit the other shapes round them.

16 Make some leaves from 11cm (4¼in) strips in various shades of brown, and glue either side of the squirrel to finish.

Red Squirrel

To make this variation (right, and opposite below), use 3mm (¹⁄₈in) strips in reddish brown, white and pale pink; 5mm (¼in) strips in reddish brown and brown. Make as for the grey squirrel, except for the ears. Make a coned peg (travel down the quilling tool, rather than rolling the paper on itself) from a 5.5cm (2¼in) strip of reddish brown. Flatten the peg slightly. Cut a fringe into a 7.5cm (3in) strip of 3mm (¹⁄₈in) reddish brown paper and roll the fringing around the cone. Make another ear and assemble all the sections as for the grey squirrel.

Mouse

Materials:

Quilling papers: 3mm
($\frac{1}{8}$in) strips in light
grey and pale pink;
2mm ($\frac{1}{16}$in) strips in
black and dark grey

Pale yellow
background card

Yellow chalk pastel

Tools:

Quilling tool

Small, sharp scissors

PVA glue

Ruler

Instructions:

1 To make the head, join three 45cm (17¾in)
light grey strips end to end and roll into a tight
coil. Push up into a dome shape. Coat the
underside of the coil with glue and allow to dry.

2 For the eyes, make two 4cm (1½in) black pegs.

3 To make the nose, roll a 5.5cm (2¼in) pale
pink strip and make into a heart shape. Cut into
a 2mm ($\frac{1}{16}$in) dark grey strip at both ends to
make whiskers.

4 For each ear, join a 22.5cm (8⅞in) pale pink
strip to a 22.5cm (8⅞in) light grey strip. Roll
up from the pink end. Make the coil into an
eccentric circle and pinch into an ear shape
as shown.

5 To make the upper body, join four 45cm
(17¾in) strips end to end, roll and push up
into a dome shape as with the head, until it
measures 2cm (¾in) high. Coat the underside
of the coil with glue and allow to dry.

6 To make the lower body, repeat step 5, but
push up the coil to measure 1.5cm (½in) high.
Coat the underside with glue and allow to dry.

7 Glue the upper and lower parts of the body
together, then glue a strip around the middle
to disguise the join.

8 For the arms and feet, make four petal
shapes from 22.5cm (8⅞in) strips.

9 To make the tail, make a very loose coil using
a 45cm (17¾in) strip. Pinch it hard into a long,
thin strip with a bend in it.

10 To assemble, shade the background card
with the chalk pastel and glue the body and
head to the card. Then attach the arms, feet,
ears and tail. Finally, add the mouse's features
to finish.

Place Setting

*To make the alternative brown mouse
place setting (opposite above),
substitute mid-brown for the light grey
paper and glue the finished mouse to a
folded piece of stiff, good-quality card.*

Giraffe

Materials:

Quilling papers: 3mm (1/8in) strips in corn and dark brown; 2mm (1/16in) strips in mid-brown and black; 5mm (1/4in) strips in dark brown

Beige background card

Pink chalk pastel

Tools:

Quilling tool

Small, sharp scissors

PVA glue

Ruler

Cocktail stick

Instructions:

1 For the single giraffe, make a loose coil from a 45cm (17¾in) corn strip for the head. Pinch into an oval shape.

2 For the neck, make eight leaf shapes using 22.5cm (8⁷/₈in) corn strips.

3 For the ears, make two teardrops from 11cm (4¼in) corn strips.

4 Make a peg from a 5.5cm (2¼in) black strip of 2mm (1/16in) paper for the eye. For the mouth, glue two short black strips together and shape into a curve.

5 For the horns, make two solid pegs from 11cm (4¼in) corn strips. Glue three short strips together to make a firmer strip. Trim to size.

6 Make five large petal shapes from 30cm (11¾in) corn strips for the body.

7 For the tail, make a long, thin triangle from a 15cm (6in) corn strip. Make a length of fringing 2cm (¾in) long from a 5mm (¼in) dark brown strip. Roll up, glue and tease out when dry.

8 To make the legs, wind a length of 3mm (1/8in) corn strip diagonally around a cocktail stick. Carefully remove and pull to tighten. Cut into sections for the legs.

9 For the hooves, make four semicircles from 11cm (4¼in) corn strips. Make four 11cm (4¼in) squashed ovals in dark brown, which will be glued on their sides.

10 Make a length of fringing from a 5mm (¼in) wide strip of dark brown to fit the length of the giraffe's neck.

11 For the giraffe's markings, make approximately eighteen random shapes from 7.5cm (3in) mid-brown 2mm (1/16in) wide strips.

12 To assemble, glue down the head, neck and body shapes onto the background card, and then glue a corn strip all round to define the shape. Glue down the ears, horns, legs and hooves. Add the brown markings, neck fringe and tail to complete.

Wedding Card

To make an alternative wedding or Valentine's card, make as for the single giraffe, but use twelve sections for the neck, and curve round to form half a heart shape. Make another giraffe in reverse. Make a bow and bow tie from two 7.5cm (3in) triangles in 3mm (⅛in) red strips. Shade the background card with pink chalk pastel.

Hedgehog

Materials:

Quilling papers: 3mm (¹/₈in) strips in brown, pastel pink and black; 5mm (¼in) strips in light brown and mid-brown; 2mm (¹/₁₆in) strips in green

Pale green background card

Green chalk pastel

Tools:

Quilling tool

Small, sharp scissors

PVA glue

Ruler

Instructions:

1 For the body of the walking hedgehog, make approximately twenty pointed fringed flowers (see page 7) from two 7.5cm (3in) strips in light and mid-brown rolled together.

2 To make the head, join a 45cm (17¾in) brown strip to a 22.5cm (8⁷/₈in) brown strip. Roll into a large coil and then pinch into a curved triangle.

3 Make pegs from a 5.5cm (2¼in) black strip for the eye and a 5.5cm (2¼in) pastel pink strip for the nose.

4 For the feet, make two petal shapes from 11cm (4¼in) brown strips.

5 To assemble, place the fringed flowers on the shaded background card close together to get the general shape, then glue them down. The flowers will merge together better once they are secured. Then glue on the head, eye and nose. Glue the feet under the fringed flowers.

6 Make seven leaf shapes from 15cm (6in) green strips. Make six leaf shapes from 11cm (4¼in) green strips. Glue two green strips together to make a firmer strip for the stem (make two stems). Roll at one end, then curve round to fit under the hedgehog. Glue down the stems, then add the leaves as shown.

Alternative Hedgehog

To make the rolled-up hedgehog (opposite, top), you will need 3mm (¹/₈in) strips in cream, pastel pink and black, 5mm (¼in) strips in light brown and mid-brown and 2mm (¹/₁₆in) strips in black. For the face, make approximately sixteen standard fringed flowers from 7.5cm (3in) cream strips. For the body, make approximately twenty-six pointed fringed flowers as above. Make two 5.5cm (2¼in) pegs from 2mm (¹/₁₆in) black strips for the eyes. Make a domed solid coil from a 11cm (4¼in) strip of 3mm (¹/₈in) pastel pink for the nose. Make two 7.5cm (3in) rounded 'v' shapes, and one 5.5cm (2¼in) semicircle for each paw. Glue them together. To assemble, arrange all fringed flowers on the shaded background card before sticking them down. Add the eyes, nose and paws to finish the design.

Reindeer

Materials:

Quilling papers: 3mm (¹/₈in) strips in mid-brown, black, white and red; 5mm (¼in) strips in mid-brown

Beige background card

Brown chalk pastel

Tools:

Quilling tool

Small, sharp scissors

PVA glue

Ruler

Instructions:

1 To make the head, make thirty fringed flowers (see page 7) from 11cm (4¼in) strips of 5mm (¼in) mid-brown paper.

2 For the eyes, make two 7.5cm (3in) black pegs, then join on 11cm (4¼in) white strips. Carry on rolling to make an oval shape.

3 For the nose, make a solid coil by rolling up a 45cm (17¾in) red strip with your fingers. Push into a slight dome and coat the underside with glue, then allow to dry.

4 To make the mouth, roll a coil from an 11cm (4¼in) red strip, and pinch into a very thin crescent shape.

5 For the main 'stems' of the antlers, make two very loose coils from 45cm (17¾in) mid-brown strips 3mm (¹/₈in) wide. Try to distribute the fullness of the paper evenly along the coil, before pinching it into a long, thin slightly curved shape. You may need to put a little glue on the back of the coil to keep the shape from opening up.

6 For the smaller 'branches' of the antlers, make six loose coils from 15cm (6in) mid-brown strips 3mm (¹/₈in) wide. Again, pinch into slightly curved thin shapes. Make two more coils from 7.5cm (3in) mid-brown strips and shape.

7 Make two coils from 15cm (6in) mid-brown strips 3mm (¹/₈in) wide and pinch at both ends for the ears.

8 To assemble the reindeer, shade the background card with the chalk pastel and then glue down the fringed flowers close together to form the head shape as follows: three flowers on the first three rows; four flowers on the fourth row; five flowers on the fifth and sixth rows; four flowers on the seventh row; and three flowers on the eighth row.

9 Glue on the reindeer's features and then the antlers, beginning with the large 'stem' shapes and then finishing with the smaller 'branches'.

Koala Bears

Materials:

Quilling papers: 3mm (¹/₈in) strips in light grey, black, brown and green; 5mm (¼in) strips in light grey and white (for the ears only)

Pale green background card

Green chalk pastel

Tools:

Quilling tool

Small, sharp scissors

PVA glue

Ruler

Instructions:

1 To make the large koala, join two 45cm (17¾in) light grey strips end to end and add a 22.5cm (8⁷/₈in) light grey strip. Roll into a large coil and make into an eccentric circle for the head.

2 For the nose, make a coil from a 22.5cm (8⁷/₈in) strip. Pinch into an oval shape.

3 Make two 5.5cm (2¼in) black pegs for the eyes.

4 For the ears, make two fringed flowers (see page 7) from two 5mm (¼in) strips in grey and white, each 5.5cm (2¼in) in length. Insert both strips into the quilling tool and roll together.

5 To make the body, join two 45cm (17¾in) light grey strips end to end and roll into a large coil. Put to one side.

6 Roll a coil using a 30cm (11¾in) light grey strip and pinch into a curved shape for the arm.

7 For the upper leg, roll a 45cm (17¾in) light grey strip into a large eccentric circle.

8 For the lower leg, roll a coil using a 22.5cm (8⁷/₈in) light grey strip, into an eccentric circle.

9 To make the lower body, make a shaped triangle from a 15cm (6in) strip.

10 To make the baby koala, roll a 45cm (17¾in) light grey strip into a coil, and make into an eccentric circle for the head.

11 Using light grey for the body, join a 45cm (17¾in) strip to a 22.5cm (8⁷/₈in) strip end to end, and roll into a coil. Make into an eccentric circle.

12 Make a 15cm (6in) light grey coil for the leg.

13 Roll a 22.5cm (8⁷/₈in) light grey coil then pinch into a curved shape for the arm.

14 For the nose, make a 7.5cm (3in) oval from a black strip.

15 Make two 3cm (1¼in) black pegs for the eyes.

16 For the ears, make two 8cm (3¼in) fringed flowers from two 5mm (¼in) strips in light grey and white, each 4cm (1½in) in length. Insert both strips into the quilling tool and roll together.

17 Shade the background card, then begin to assemble the heads and bodies of the koalas. Fit the larger koala body around the other shapes. Glue both arms on top of the bodies, and also the lower legs as shown.

18 For the branch, make ten 15cm (6in) petal shapes from brown strips. Make nine 11cm (4¼in) coils in green and pinch into pointed shapes for the leaves. Glue down in groups of three on the branch as shown.

Dancing Bear

Materials:

Quilling papers: 3mm
(¹/₈in) strips in black,
white, brown and gold
with a gold edge; 2mm
(¹/₁₆in) strips in white
(for the bow tie only)

Small square of black
tissue paper

Scrap of gold paper

Beige background card

Yellow chalk pastel

Tools:

Quilling tool

Small, sharp
scissors

PVA glue

Ruler

Fine black pen

Glass-headed pin

Instructions:

1 To make the head, join together four 45cm (17¾in) brown strips end to end. Roll into a large peg.

2 For the muzzle, make a solid coil from a 22.5cm (8⁷/₈in) brown strip. Push up into a dome using a glass-headed pin or similar. Coat the underside of the coil with glue and allow to dry. Glue this to the centre of the head and carefully draw on the features with a fine black pen.

3 Make two semicircles from 11cm (4¼in) brown strips for the ears.

4 For the hat, make a rectangle from a 30cm (11¾in) black strip, rolled into a coil and pinched into shape, curved slightly at one end to fit the brim.

5 To make the hat brim, glue three short black strips together to make a firmer strip. Curve slightly and trim to size.

6 For the body, glue a 45cm (17¾in) white strip to a 15cm (6in) white strip. Do the same with some brown strips, then glue the end of the white strip to the end of the brown strip. Begin to roll from the white end to make a large coil. Make this into an eccentric circle.

7 To make the arms, make two rectangles from 30cm (11¾in) black strips. Shape them at one short end to fit the sides of the body.

8 Make two semicircles from 11cm (4¼in) brown strips for the paws.

9 To make the legs, glue a 45cm (17¾in) brown strip to a 15cm (6in) brown strip. Roll the whole strip to form a large coil. Pinch into a teardrop, then move along from this point and pinch again to make the top of the leg. Finally, pinch the other end to form the foot. Repeat this to make the other leg.

10 For the sides of the jacket, make two thin crescents from 22.5cm (8⁷/₈in) black strips.

11 To make the coat tails, make two thin shapes as shown, using 22.5cm (8⁷/₈in) black strips.

12 For the bow tie, make two triangles from 7.5cm (3in) strips of 2mm (¹/₁₆in) white paper. Use a small square of 2mm (¹/₁₆in) strip in white for the knot and glue to the centre of the bow tie.

13 For the cane, cut a 5cm (2in) square of black tissue paper. Roll it diagonally around a cocktail stick. Glue down the point and carefully remove the cocktail stick. Trim to 4cm (1½in) in length. Glue a short strip of gold card around the top.

14 To make the stars, fold a gold-edged strip into a zigzag – make a glue tab at one end, then fold five full points before trimming. Pull round into a ring, and glue the tab into the first point. Even out the points to complete the star.

15 Shade the background card with the chalk pastel and then arrange the bear on it. Glue everything in place, beginning with the head. Glue the cane under his paw and add a number of stars to complete the design.

Acknowledgements

Diane would like to thank everyone at
Search Press for bringing *Quilled Animals*
to life – especially May Corfield for her support
and expert editing, and Paul Bricknell for
such amazing photography, which really
captures the essence of quilling.

Publisher's Note

You are invited to visit the
author's website:
www.jjquilling.co.uk